Laid Down

Laid Down

A 30-Day Devotional for the Woman
Longing for Rest

Cathy Harris

Laid Down
A 30-Day Devotional for the Woman Longing for Rest
© 2018 by Cathy Harris
All rights reserved.

Published in The United States

ISBN-13: 978-0692067291

ISBN-10: 0692067299

In honor of women who daily and faithfully lay their lives down for others.

CONTENTS

Welcome

There is no better feeling than the warm and cozy shalom I feel when I pull up my bed covers over my chilled body on a cold rainy morning. I look at the clock, and I discover I've been blessed with another hour to rest. This doesn't happen often in my house with three little ones who boldly arise with the sun, but when it does, it breathes life into this often tired mother. If only I had a coffee maker in my room to add to that extra hour in my bed, that would be the cherry on top.

Our life in God is better than the extra hour in bed with a warm cup of coffee. Even on the most exhausting days when life has just wrung us out like an old wet rag, Jesus brings life and life to the fullest. We may know this, but do we always live in this reality? We are all broken people confined to an earthly flesh suit that can only take on so much. We so easily get weighed down and physically, mentally, and emotionally fatigued by life's burdens. As I juggle being a homeschool mom, a wife, a writer, an educator, and just little me, I often end the day barely able to keep my eyes open. Although I am thankful for this abundant season, my life is full.

There have also been seasons in my life when it was much harder to breathe. For example, there were months in my first year of marriage when we experienced unemployment with a new baby. My worry and fear blinded me from the life available to me in God. Peace trailed far behind me, and rest never seemed to have a chance to keep up. I longed for some sense of control and the ability to make things right, but I came up short.

We all have our stories; maybe you are in the midst of an unyielding story right now. Or, maybe you are just trying to be faithful with all your everyday responsibilities, and it feels like you are drowning. As we search the scriptures together for the next 30-days, I pray you will find your story in the midst of God's unraveling kingdom story. I pray you will find yourself, your home, and your resting place in His Word.

Living in rest is not always easy, yet it is consistently available. Often, we must diligently seek it, but it is there to enjoy. Finding rest has been one of the most challenging and intentional journeys I have taken with the Lord. Jesus has helped me to treasure rest, and I am honored to walk with you as you begin or continue your journey to find rest yourself. So, feel free to lay down, pull-up those covers, and enjoy God, because He wants to enjoy you.

Each of the daily devotionals in this book consists of a scripture verse, suggested reading that puts the verse in context, a short encouragement or teaching, four reflection questions, an activation prayer, and a space for you to journal. I encourage you to soak it all in. Meditate on the scriptures, pray through the teaching and consider how it applies to you. Answer the reflection questions honestly and believe God for breakthrough as you pray each activation prayer!

Because I know you are busy, the devotional is set up to take you about 15 minutes a day, although you can dive in and spend as much time as you'd like. You can also grab a few friends to do it with you.

The reflection questions are framed in such a way for you to go deeper with your small group or Bible study group.

My hope is that this devotional will be a memorial stone in your life. I pray that as you look back on these intentional 30 days, you will remember the moments God met you and led you to your resting place in Him. Devote yourself to Him, and He will give you your inheritance. You are His daughter, and He longs to meet with you.

"Greater love has no one than this, that he lay down his life for his friends."

John 15:13

Day 1

Promise & Invitation

"Come to me, all you who are weary and heavy-laden, and I will give you rest. Take my yoke upon you and learn from me, for I am gentle and humble in heart, and you will find rest for your souls. For my yoke is easy and my burden is light."

Matthew 11: 28-30 (NAS)

Read Matthew 11:25-30

Come and rest. The Christian life is not promised to be easy, but Jesus looks upon us with compassion. He sees us running hard, serving Him well, and loving those He brings into our circle. He discerns the burdens of life lying heavy on our shoulders, and He sees our desire to find His easy yoke. Just as His disciples were, we are often like infants learning how to walk in grace. The journey is full of joy, yet it is also often overwhelming. To those who get tired along the way, Jesus promises rest.

We will find rest when we come to Him. Burdens are harsh, life-stealing, and demanding. On the contrary, Jesus is a kind gentleman. He invites you into His house. His rooms are full of joy, peace, and stillness. He says, "Take my yoke upon you and learn from me." In other words, "Let me lead you in your everyday adventures, demands, responsibilities, and desires. We are connected, and I hold the reins. I will not jerk you from side to side. Learn from me, and I will teach you how to live in rest." Will you accept His invitation?

We can walk with Jesus in the cool of the day as two honeymoon lovers. It does not mean life will be effortless. In fact, it can often be burdensome. If we trust Him, we can live supernaturally. Can you imagine what it would be like to live from a place of rest in your soul? A soul at rest is absent from worry, fear, anxiety, selfish ambition, and striving. A soul at rest in God knows who she is and whose she is. We live in the world, but the world does not have to live in us. The kingdom of God operates by a radically different system.

Some of us need to speak a word of peace to our souls today. You can declare the promises of God over your life. When we proclaim it, our faith arises. Next thing we know, we are walking out those declarations.

Reflection:

1. Do you have burdens that are difficult to give to Jesus?

2. What does it mean to you to learn from Jesus?

3. How can you accept Jesus' invitation into rest today?

4. Write down two bold declarations for yourself today.

Activation Prayer:

Jesus, thank you for your promises. Help me to learn from you today. Thank you that I do not have to figure out life on my own. You are my faithful Shepherd, so I take your yoke upon me today. I choose to rest with you.

Journal:

Day 2

A Quiet Place

"Then, because so many people were coming and going that they
did not even have a chance to eat, he said to them, "Come with me
by yourselves to a quiet place and get some rest."

Mark 6:31 (NIV)

Read Mark 6

Jesus sent the disciples out to do the works of the Kingdom of God.
He gave them authority, instruction, and each other to link arms.
They were healing the sick, casting out demons, and preaching the
gospel (Acts 6:12-13). Their work consisted of long and demanding
days with little time to eat or sleep. Naturally, they came back to
Jesus worn out and hungry. He saw it on their faces. The work of the
kingdom for these men was demanding. The people were desperate
for every ounce of glory to be released from them. The excitement
for the Holy Spirit's work was contagious. The disciples chose to
pour themselves out like a drink offering.

You and I may not be sent to cast out demons on a daily basis, but we all have our marching orders. What are the instructions Jesus has given you today? Instead of people desperate for healing all around you, you may have small children desperate for your attention. Can you relate to the disciples who did not have time to care for themselves in the midst of their ministry? Does it remind you of motherhood? Can you imagine Jesus taking your hand and leading you to a quiet place to eat and rest as He did for the disciples?

You might not get a chance to eat alone today, yet we can pray that He meets you in your quiet time with Him. Jesus encounters those who seek Him in the time they have, even if it is short. We want to be careful not to make "life" an excuse not to sit with Him. In your honest pursuit of Him, trust Him to meet you. There is a feast prepared for you in His presence. He sits at the right hand of God and provides pleasures forever (Ps. 16:11). His luxuries are far better than the earthly gratifications that pursue our hearts.

I challenge you today to choose Him over your phone or that next TV show. Sit for a moment, meditate on His goodness, or even take a nap. Give Him your burdens again. Let today's worries and to-dos fade into the background of His voice. Fight for the quiet in your heart today. He wants to meet with you.

Reflection:

1. When is the best time for you to have quiet time with the Lord?

2. Are there other activities consistently stealing your time from the Lord?

3. If Jesus personally pulled you away with Him for a few minutes, how would you spend that time?

4. How can you take care of yourself today?

Activation Prayer:

Speak to me today, Holy Spirit, and lead me to Jesus. Make known to me the mysteries of the Kingdom and help me to walk them out. Help me feel your pursuit gently nudging me to the quiet place with you.

Journal:

Day 3

Our Shaken Boats

"The disciples went and woke him, saying, "Master, Master, we're going to drown!" He got up and rebuked the wind and the raging waters; the storm subsided, and all was calm."

Luke 8:24 (NIV)

Read Luke 8:22-25

Even in the midst of the raging sea, Jesus is calm. Nothing rocks His boat. Nothing is unexpected. Jesus may not get billowed, but we most certainly do. We are so often just as fearful as the disciples were. We hang on to His coat sleeves yelling, "Jesus, we are going to drown!" As the waves rock our boat from side to side, we stumble, fall, get hurt, become discouraged, and maybe even become a little hopeless or angry.

This story reminds me of our brokenness as human beings. The disciples had been with Jesus. They witnessed miracle after miracle, yet they still questioned His response to the storm. They knew He could calm the seas, but they had not learned why He calms the seas. Or, why He might wait to calm the seas. Despite the disciple's frustration and desperation, Jesus was there. The Word tells us that Jesus only did what He saw the Father doing and said what the Father spoke to Him (John 5:19). Therefore, as Jesus rested, He also trusted. Jesus held the power to calm the seas but waited until given the instruction. He demonstrated faith. He taught them how to rest even in the midst of the storm.

Faith means we surrender authority to Him to calm our storm according to His wisdom. He wants us to learn from Him while life is still moving. He says, "See how I am calm and at rest? I want you to do the same." Time will continue to advance at its fast pace, storms will progress around us, and there will be times we are overwhelmed. It is how we respond in those uncertain moments that have the power to bring peace and rest.

Rather than reacting to the seas, follow Jesus' lead. In this passage, Jesus extended an invitation to His disciples to believe Him for rest in the midst of uncertainty and turmoil. Will you accept the invitation?

Reflection:

1. Are there storms raging around you that make it hard to see Jesus?

2. Do you feel like you are drowning or floating on the waves?

3. How will you practically choose to rest (follow Jesus' lead) today?

4. How is Jesus asking you to trust Him today?

Activation Prayer:

Thank you, Jesus, that you are always in control. No matter what life brings, you are at peace. I pray right now for my mind and my heart to be flooded with your peace that surpasses my understanding. Teach me how to sit with you today in the boat while the sea rages around me.

Journal:

Day 4

Teach Us to Pray

"It happened that while Jesus was praying in a certain place, after He had finished, one of His disciples said to Him, "Lord, teach us to pray just as John also taught his disciples."

Luke 11:1 (NAS)

Read Luke 11:1-4

Prayer is our conversation with God. Prayer is our communion. Jesus, our mediator, ripped the veil so that we can approach our Heavenly Father. Relationship with God is the love story of the entire Bible. In Adam and Eve's day, He walked intimately with them in the garden. After the resurrection, the Holy Spirit was given to dwell within us. Now, we look to the day Jesus will return to us and intimately live amongst us again. The passion burning on the inside of His heart is always intimacy with us. He is both Emmanuel (God with us) and Maranatha (God coming). Prayer is how this relationship cultivates mature intimacy.

Jesus taught practically on prayer and demonstrated a life of prayer to His disciples, because He knew it was the only way to rest with the Father and to know the Father's will. He knew what was on the horizon for these friends of His. He taught them to prioritize communion in prayer before things got dicey.

In an intimate relationship, we understand the importance of communicating and spending time together. Intentionally investing in one another is the only way we go deeper into our relationship. Our friendship with Jesus works just the same way. When we spend time with Him, we get to know Him. The more time we spend with Him, the more intimately acquainted with His desires, His passions, and His heartbreaks we become. Do you have a friend whom you know so well that you know what will encourage their heart? I cherish these friendships. We can be this intimate with Jesus. The closer we get, the more we know His character.

Prayer is often petitioning or asking for something, but the essence of prayer is communion. Over time, life becomes more of an adventure with Jesus than a mundane obligation. Though sometimes tiring, adventures bring joy, rest, and purpose. Today, I encourage you to read through the rest of the Lord's prayer found in Luke 11. Spend time meditating on each line. Jesus is the master teacher. Let's hang on every word that comes forth from His mouth.

Reflection:

1. What does it look like for God's kingdom to come in your life?

2. Is it difficult to trust God for your daily bread (needs)?

3. What facet of God's character do you desire to get to know more in prayer?

4. How can you commune with God as you go about your daily life today?

Activation Prayer:

Jesus, I ask you to teach me how to pray. Ignite the desire within me to sit with you and enjoy your company. I desire to know you more and rest in who you are and always will be. Remind me today of your unfailing love and your passion for being with me.

Journal:

Day 5

More Than Enough

"Jesus called His disciples to Him and said, "I have compassion for these people; they have already been with Me three days and have nothing to eat. I do not want to send them away hungry, or they may collapse on the way."

Matthew 15:32 (NIV)

Read Matthew 15:29-39

A large crowd anxiously gathers around Jesus. They are looking over each other's shoulders to get a glimpse of Him at work. He has already healed a multitude of people. For hours, the crowd watches with anticipation. Miracle after miracle fills their hungry souls. Of course, who has time to eat during a time like this? Then the intensity dies down, and Jesus looks out on the crowd with compassion.

After hours of ministry, He wants to fill their now hungry bellies before their long journey back home. Though He could have easily and miraculously fed them by Himself in an instant, He invites His disciples to set the table. This request is no small task. Jesus has invited 5,000 people to dinner!

In the natural sense, there was not enough food to go around. Jesus was well aware of this, but He saw beyond the natural into the supernatural. The disciples, on the other hand, could not see past their lack. I imagine I would respond in the same way. I get overwhelmed when I have to prepare a meal for just a few extra people. Days of planning, grocery store shopping, and cleaning anxiously unfold. Hospitality does not come easily for me. It actually takes a lot of my energy. Do you think the disciples had the gift of hospitality? Nevertheless, Jesus asks them to host 5,000 people immediately, and He asks them to do it well.

Jesus begins the feast with a declaration, "There is always more than enough." They all needed to hear this truth, and so do we. He doesn't want us burning out and collapsing along our journey. There is always enough at the table whether we are the ones serving the food or eating the food. Despite this, many of us live from a place of lack. We convince ourselves there just isn't enough available for us or for those to whom we minister. We may believe we lack money, clothes, prestige, favor, or even time. Just like the disciples, we can become so accustomed to living in a place of lack that we can't see the miracles He performs around us. He has prepared a spacious place for us to live and invite others into.

Our stress, worry, doubt, and fear all stem from the belief that there is not enough for us at the table. Sister, I assure you, there is always enough for you at God's table. You can rest, cease your striving, and know that He is God. May you have eyes to see beyond the natural resources today into the supernatural resources available to you and others you serve. Your first step is faith. Be brave today.

Reflection:

1. Do you find it hard to believe there is more than enough for you?

2. What fears or worries do you need to lay down before God today?

3. How will you choose to live from a place of promise instead of lack?

4. What do you believe God will provide? Are you dreaming beyond your available resources?

Activation Prayer:

Jesus, I praise you and thank you that you are more than enough for me. I rest knowing that you are holding me up and providing for my every need. You care about every need in my life. Help me to be still before you and let you be God.

Journal:

Day 6

A Warrior's Joy

"The Lord, your God, is in your midst, a victorious warrior. He will exult over you with joy; He will quiet you in His love, He will rejoice over you with shouts of joy."

Zephaniah 3:17 (NAS)

Read Zephaniah 3:12-20

Even in the day of judgment, God will sing with joy over His bride. Jesus took on the cross for the joy set before Him. He took on judgment and joy simultaneously. He is both just and righteous. He is always kind to correct us while also rejoicing over us. It is important to remember that He desires that we would become like Jesus. His vision is beautiful, and He will do whatever it takes to get us there. He knows we are broken people, and we desperately need His help to walk in maturity.

We all have room in our life for further growth. If we ever think we have reached the pinnacle of learning from God, we are profoundly mistaken. Sometimes, these seasons of learning involve deep correction, repentance, and paradigm shifts. Other times, our learning opportunities may look like kind correction from the Holy Spirit when we yell at our kids, judge a coworker for their actions, or hold a record of wrong when our spouse disappoints us.

The Holy Spirit is faithful to reveal the truth, lead us in kindness to repentance, and make the mysteries of Heaven known to us. The more we listen to and learn from the Holy Spirit, the more like Jesus we become. Jesus did not come to condemn the world or overwhelm you with all your mistakes and failures (John 3:17). He came to bring you abundant life.

Zephaniah, although still under the Old Covenant, believed and proclaimed these truths of God. He prophesied both judgment and the restoration of Judah. He understood and took on a portion of God's great love for His people. He watched as the people of God turned from Him, sinned against Him, and forgot their first love, yet he longed for them to learn from the Lord and mature in love.

Life doesn't always work out the way we hoped it would. We don't always choose the "holy route" in all our decisions. All of us have heartaches, pains, and experiences we cannot explain. Our own choices and unexplainable circumstances can both zap our joy and steal our rest. Nevertheless, He is there. Through it all, His love song resounds in our ears. Despite the exhaustion, failure, or confusion, I challenge you to take the chance and sing with Him today. Worship Him anyway, and let the peace of God guard your heart and your mind (Phil. 4:7).

Reflection:

1. Do you need to know and experience God's might today?

2. Is there restoration that needs to take place in an area of your life?

3. Take a moment to thank God for the ways He has displayed His might in your life.

4. Have you ever mistaken the Lord's kind correction for punishment or abandonment? Write down the situation, and ask Him to speak to you as you write.

Activation Prayer:

Jesus, even though I may not always understand your ways, help me to worship you in the midst of the battle. Help me to hear you singing over me. Help me rest in your love and joy. Thank you that you light my path and are faithful to reveal any self-indulgent way in my heart. Lead me by your kindness and make me more like you.

Journal:

Day 7

Labor to Rest

"Let us labor therefore to enter into that rest, lest any man falls after the same example of unbelief. For the word of God is quick, and powerful, and sharper than any two-edged sword, piercing even to the dividing asunder of soul and spirit, and of the joints and marrow, and is a discerner of the thoughts and intents of the heart."

Hebrews 4:11-12 (KJV)

Read Hebrews 4:1-16

Let us labor to enter rest. The Greek word for labor in the text is *spoudazō*, meaning to hasten, to be diligent, or to exert one's self. The author urges us to make a valiant effort to rest, lest our work will begin to cause unbelief and falsehood in our hearts. This exhortation is astounding and challenges our logic. Furthermore, when we continue reading the next verse, we quickly understand its immense importance. "The Word of God is living and active" (Heb. 4:12). The author seems to relate rest and the diligent seeking of rest to the receipt of truth and God's word in our lives. We cannot receive truth when worry fear, anxiety, or anything else that opposes His nature consume our mind.

We may naturally think that rest means abstaining from moving forward or sacrificing a finished product. In fact, diligently pursuing rest keeps our efforts at the feet of Jesus and our physical body from exhaustion. Much more can be accomplished in rest and surrender to His ways in one day than all the work and striving for one hundred days. For He can do far more than we could ever ask or imagine (Eph. 3:20). He has divine strategies, wisdom, clarity, and grace to release. Rest opens our hands to receive His gifts.

Rest is an act of trust. We trust God enough that if we take time for Him, our family, to sleep, or even just to take care of ourselves that everything will still be ok. We trust that His good gifts will be released. Resting is relinquishing control and loosening our grip on our lives. I encourage you to lay down your to-do list or even your goals and dreams before Him today. Take an hour or even a day to rest. Seek Him and see how He moves.

This exhortation reminds me of the First Thanksgiving story. Days of worry without rain and laborious efforts in the fields ended with one day of prayer and rest. If God did not show up, all their crops were at risk, but they took a chance. They trusted His character. And, it seemed it was the only choice they had. All their work and striving were not even making a dent. They were desperate, so they rested. In a day of famine and drought, they trusted God with their lives and their children's lives. We all know how the story ends. One day of rest and prayer led to an abundance of rain and crops. He did exceeding more than they asked. For that, they were thankful.

Reflection:

1. Is physical rest difficult for you? Why? Commit to rest for a short period of time today or several days.

2. What are your to-dos, worries, or goals that are hardest to lay at the Lord's feet?

3. Do you believe that God is willing to work on your behalf? Is it difficult to trust Him?

4. What are you entrusting to God right now? Do you believe He will abundantly provide?

Activation Prayer:

Help me to rest with you today. I ask you to show me when you are calling me to lay down my hands and head. Thank you that you are in control, and you are always moving on my behalf.

Journal:

Day 8

The Good Shepherd

"He makes me lie down in green pastures. He leads me beside the quiet waters."

Psalm 23:2 (NAS)

Read Psalm 23

The Lord is our good Shepherd. He "makes" us lie down and "leads" us beside quiet waters. If you are anything like me, especially when I am anxious, it is a struggle to rest. I need the Lord to gently "make" me lie down. He faithfully reminds me through my sweet husband who gently urges me to stop cleaning and sit down with him. God reminds me to rest through my children who ask me to set aside a writing project to read them a book.

He makes us lie down, but it is a gentle nudge. He sees us working and exhausting ourselves. He waits for that sweet moment to take our hand, speak peace, and invite us into His presence. When we follow His lead, stillness is our destination. Even when the storm still rages, the dishes consistently pile up, and the deadlines are fast approaching, the waters of our souls can rest in God. Stillness takes practice, yielding, and a whole lot of trust.

When we rest, we also find delicious fruit. God does not ask us to sit and dwell in the midst of our mess or turmoil. He brings us to His banqueting table. Just as a shepherd leads his sheep to the greenest pastures, our Jesus leads us to a place in Him that is far better and fruitful than any home the world could offer. He knows the way to get to the greenest pastures. I imagine as a shepherd leads his sheep to the chosen field, they often try to wonder in their craved direction. It might be similar to guiding young children through the grocery store. Everything along the way catches their eye.

A good shepherd leads his sheep with his rod. He gently holds it out or nudges them to go in the right direction. The sheep trust him and know his voice, so they follow (John 10:27). Jesus leads us in the same way. We feel His gentle nudge when we start veering off His path. But, we can trust He always has the best pasture waiting for us. His prod is not to condemn us. Let Him be your guide. He knows the way to the greenest pastures and the waters you desire for refreshing.

Even when you do not see the end to all the hustle and bustle in sight, He says, "Oh my dear, it is only the beginning for me and you." There are beautiful times, Jesus is asking us to serve faithfully as Martha did, but there are also times He calls us to sit before Him like Mary did. We need His wisdom to bring balance in our lives lest we burn out.

Reflection:

1. Do you often hear God's gentle encouragement to rest?

2. What would it look for you to listen to His leading when He "makes" you lie down?

3. Meditate on "quiet waters." What does this mean to you?

4. Where are you on your journey? Do you feel like you are still waiting to find the green pastures, or have you already set up your picnic with Him beside the waters?

Activation Prayer:

Thank you, Jesus, for being my good shepherd. Help me to follow your lead. Today, I yield to you and follow you to my green pastures and quiet waters. I want to live in the places you have prepared for me. Your presence restores my soul, so your presence is where I want to remain.

Journal:

Day 9

The Sabbath Rest

"By the seventh day God completed His work which He had done, and He rested on the seventh day of all His work which He had done."

Genesis 2:2 (NAS)

Read Genesis 2:1-4

God rested. This statement is profound. He is the One who holds the universe, creates the ocean's boundaries, and knows you in and through. He created the Heavens and the Earth, yet He never tired. If He never tired, why do you think God chose to rest? He not only rested, but He blessed and sanctified the seventh day of creation as a day of rest. He rested not because He was tired. He rested for His pleasure and enjoyment. He rested to enjoy humanity, the apple of His eye. These are the reasons for the Sabbath rest.

According to the Law, all work ceased on the Sabbath (Ex. 20:10). It was and still is a day of rest and enjoyment. The Sabbath, according to the Jewish custom, is a day sanctified and dedicated to the Lord (Deut. 5:14). It is also a day to enjoy family. After spending some time in Israel a few years ago, I came to love and look forward to the Sabbath. Every Friday evening as the sun went down, we prepared for our meal together. It was a time to sit around the table and speak blessing over each other. Fathers intentionally take the time to bless each of their children at the dinner table. The depth and intentionality are incredible and life-giving.

Jesus came to fulfill the law. He is the Lord of the Sabbath (Matt. 12:8). Therefore, keeping the Sabbath is no longer about fulfilling the law or offering a sacrifice to the Lord. He is not looking for our sacrifice, but He is looking for our compassion, rest, and intimacy with Him (Matt. 12:7). Keeping the Sabbath is holy, purposeful, and fruitful. It is intentional time for renewal.

Keeping the Sabbath may look different for each of us. Setting aside an entire day may not be feasible in your season, but devoting a dedicated and consistent time to rest is wise. It is wise and intimate to lay back on Jesus' bosom to listen while your hands stay still. It is an investment in your relationship with God and those around you. The world will keep spinning, but we have to stop and receive the breath of life. If God rested, so must we.

Reflection:

1. What does keeping the Sabbath mean to you?

2. Is there a day or part of the day you could set aside for your Sabbath rest?

3. What are practical ways you could prepare for and diligently enter into a Sabbath rest?

4. How could you intentionally invest in your relationship with God and others during a Sabbath rest?

Activation Prayer:

God, I ask you to guide me into your Sabbath rest. Show me how and when I can be diligent to enter into the rest you have prepared for me. Help me to trust you and lean on you. Meet me as I draw near to you in the place of rest and bless the works of my hands.

Journal:

Day 10

His Throne of Grace

"For we do not have a high priest who is unable to empathize with our weaknesses, but we have one who has been tempted in every way, just as we are—yet He did not sin. Let us then approach God's throne of grace with confidence, so that we may receive mercy and find grace to help us in our time of need."

Hebrews 4:15-16 (NIV)

Read Hebrews 4:1-16

On the day of His resurrection, Jesus was glorified. He sits in Heavenly places at the right hand of God the Father (Acts 2:33). As our high priest, He makes constant intercession for us as the mediator between the Father and humanity (1 Tim. 2:5). Jesus walked the earth as a man to save men. He experienced weariness and desperate need for God the Father. Jesus took on flesh and physically had to lay His head to rest and cease from the daily work of His hands. He empathizes with our weakness because He experienced it Himself.

We can approach His throne with confidence. He knows our weaknesses, and He knows how to help us even when we don't know what we need. As humans when we are weak, we are often tempted to pull away from God as if we are not living up to our performance for Him. But, this is the complete opposite of what we are encouraged to do. We can draw near.

In 2 Corinthians 12:9, Paul boasts in His weakness. He recognized that He was broken and did not deserve the life He lived. He knew He was frail but understood that when he was weak Christ's strength was perfected in Him. Godly strength is perfected in us when we draw near. In the presence of God, grace extends and suddenly we have a vitality beyond understanding. When we thought we might not make it to the end of the day, we then have confidence we will thrive in hardship regardless of how long it takes.

I encourage you today to approach Him. He is not far off. He is not a distant God lording over you while watching your every wrong move. He is intimate, relatable, and near. His grace is sufficient for you (2 Cor. 12:9). Yet, He will continue to give all us more than we can handle. If we could juggle it all, we would forget our need for Him. It is the place of constant learning, hunger, and dependence where we go deeper into His heart for us.

Reflection:

1. Do you experience God's promised confidence and grace when you approach Him?

2. What does God's nearness mean to you? (Read Psalm 73:28, Psalm 145:18, Isaiah 55:6)

3. In what areas do you need God's grace today?

4. Can you boast in your weakness as Paul did, or do you shrink back and try to hide it? God wants to show Himself strong within you today.

Activation Prayer:

Jesus, I receive your grace today and rest in your presence. Help me know that you are near. I cling to you and ask you to strengthen my inner man. I have confidence that when I am weak, your strength is perfected in me.

Journal:

Day 11

Sufficient Grace

"And He said to me, 'My grace is sufficient for you, for my power is perfected in weakness.' Most gladly, therefore, I will rather boast about my weaknesses, so that the power of Christ may dwell in me."

2 Corinthians 12:9 (NAS)

Read 2 Corinthians 12:7-9

His power rests on us, or dwells in us, in our weakness. Is God's power the first thing you think of when you feel weak? I do not, but I sure wish I did. We all desperately need to receive this revelation. His grace is sufficient and abundant. When we are at our weakest, we can tap into His power. When we know we are powerful in God, we are also confident. We continue to walk in the ways of His kingdom, are not prone to fall into sin, and receive the wisdom of Heaven in our circumstances.

According to the world's structure, when we are weak, we feel defeated. We want to give up and back off from pursuing our hopes and dreams. Thankfully, Christ offers the opposite of our fleshly temptations. Grace is available. Grace is resurrected power freely given to us. Grace is supernatural strength in times of desperation and hardship. Grace is always available in every situation.

His grace is a gift, although it is our choice to live in it and receive it. His grace is perfected in us in our moments of weakness. So, next time you feel weak, declare God's grace over you. Soak in the presence of His grace and feel the strength of His love arise within you. Like Paul, we are encouraged to boast of our weakness and Christ's power. Paul even goes as far to say he is glad that he is weak!

Jesus gets all the glory when the impossible becomes possible in the midst of what you could never do on your own. It is not about what you can do. It is all about what He can do in you. We so often approach a mountain and think, "I just do not have grace to climb that today." But, in God, there is always grace. Perhaps it's not grace we lack but confidence in God's ability.

There is grace today to teach your child to read. There is grace today to stay up all night with your nursing babe. There is grace today to press into intimacy in your marriage. There is grace to perform and serve at work with excellence. His grace is sufficient for it all. Our lack of strength does not equal His lack of grace.

Reflection:

1. What are the moments you feel the weakest?

2. In what parts of your life do you need to experience an increase in of His grace?

3. What does it mean to boast of your weakness?

4. Is there a mountain in front of you that you need God's experiential grace to scale?

Activation Prayer:

I praise you, Lord, that when I am weak, you are strong. I thank you for your sufficient grace in my life. I ask that you would teach me to walk in your grace and receive your perfected power in my life. I want to experience your supernatural gladness even in the midst of my weakness.

Journal:

Day 12

Unity

"Behold, how good and pleasant it is when God's people live together in unity! It is like the precious oil poured on the head, running down on the beard, running down on Aaron's beard, down on the collar of his robe. It is as if the dew of Hermon were falling on Mount Zion. For there the Lord bestows His blessing, even life forevermore."

Psalm 133:1-3 (NIV)

Read Psalm 133

Refreshment from Heaven pours over us in the presence of believers. Shrinking back, isolation, and division are schemes of the enemy to keep us bound, worn out, and powerless. Unity is pleasing to the Lord. It is like a sweet aroma arising in Heaven that swells until blessing pours out. The oil running down Aaron's beard speaks of the priestly anointing, and the dew of Hermon represents God's mercy and refreshing. Unity is a vital component of a full life in God. Unity answers the cry of Jesus' heart. He prayed to the Father that we would be one just as Him and the Father are one (John 17:21). If Jesus longed for it, this is the way we ought to live.

Are there areas in your life where there is a division with other believers? Are you a part of a community that experiences the blessing of unity? These are vital questions for all of us to ask ourselves. We were not meant to live this life alone. Not only do we have the help of the Holy Spirit, but we have the Body of Christ. When we are weary, we so often need an Aaron or a Hur to hold our arms up as these men did for Moses (Ex. 17:12).

This kind of biblical unity requires vulnerability, faithfulness, and consistency. We have to dedicate ourselves to cultivating relationships that reflect the heart of God. We can often find these relationships in church community groups, mentorships, or even a friendship that has lasted through a few ups and downs. In whatever way these relationships develop in our lives, it is wise to give ourselves to them. God commands blessing to flow when we are unified. Fruitfulness in the form of peace, joy, and self-control are planted and birthed. It is like oil from Heaven flowing over you.

When we are tired, our relationships can naturally fall through the cracks. We struggle to find the time to meet a friend for coffee, attend the community group, or intentionally spend time with our spouse. Although this might be a temptation, the Word of God makes clear that it is in the context of relationships that we find rest, not isolation. Just because you can't commit hours to your college friend like you used to, doesn't mean you cannot have a life-giving community.

Reflection:

1. Who are the people that hold your arms up when you are tired and weak?

2. Are you a part of a community of believers that lives in unity?

3. If you are not experiencing the blessing of unity, pray now for God to bring such a community into your life. What are practical ways you could give yourself to cultivating this?

4. How can you continue or begin to invest in your relationships more intentionally?

Activation Prayer:

Jesus, thank you for your Body. I praise you that you created me to be a part of a community. I pray you will show me who those people are that I can grow with and do life with me. I ask for your blessing of unity in my life.

Journal:

Day 13
Fellowship

"Day by day continuing with one mind in the temple, and breaking bread from house to house, they were taking their meals together with gladness and sincerity of heart, praising God and having favor with all the people. And the Lord was adding to their number day by day those who were being saved."

Acts 2:46-47 (NAS)

Read Acts 2:37-47

Biblical fellowship bears fruit. When we take a look at the early church, their unity and love challenge us. They lived life together. They shared their possessions. They ate together, prayed together, and worshipped together. The love that they shared not only blessed them, but it was so unique that others took notice. Outsiders came to Jesus because of holy jealousy for Heaven's ordained community. The early church demonstrated a community that was genuine, life-giving, and contagious.

We were created for this kind of fellowship. The world longs for it. Of course, the early church was also preaching the gospel, but I love that many were coming to the Lord by their love for one another. They were not only proclaiming the gospel; they were living out the radical gospel day after day before them. Biblical fellowship is beautiful and advances the kingdom. We all have friends that we enjoy watching a movie with, but I encourage you to take a look at the relationships in which you have invested in. Are they life-giving or life-draining? When others look at your friendships, does it provoke them to holy jealousy?

Paul often refers throughout the epistles to those that refreshed him by their love and hospitality (1 Cor. 16:18). Believers ministered to him in the midst of very trying days. We all need these relationships in our lives. When I am tired, worn down, and feeling alone, a simple dinner or playdate with a good friend breathes new perspective and life into me.

Biblical fellowship brings the fruit of peace into our lives. If you are feeling desperate for rest and fruit in your life, surround yourself with friends who desire more of Jesus, and I promise you will find more of Him in their presence. Jesus said, "For where two or three are gathered, I am in their midst" (Matt. 18:20).

Reflection:

1. Are your relationships breathing life into you? Who are the people with whom you can experience life-giving fellowship?

2. How can you intentionally go deeper in your relationships to live an Acts 2 lifestyle?

3. How do you think biblical fellowship can bring rest to your life?

4. Who can you "break bread" with this week?

Activation Prayer:

Jesus, I ask for your wisdom in my relationships. Show me the relationships where I can invest myself and reveal those that do not breed life. I long to live an Acts 2 lifestyle in my community. Show me what that looks like and give me the courage to pursue it.

Journal:

Day 14

Hope

"Therefore my heart is glad, and my glory rejoices; My flesh also will rest in hope."

Psalm 16:9 (NKJV)

Read Psalm 16

Hope believes in something bigger than ourselves. Hope believes in something real even if we cannot see it or feel it. Hope believes that God is good and bigger than our circumstances. The Psalmist reminds us of the importance of a thankful and glad heart that manifests in the place of worship. We do not hope because everything is always effortless. We hope because God never changes.

When our flesh wants to dwell on our circumstances or short-comings, our heart can still enter into a place of praise. A thankful heart prepares the way for the Lord (Ps. 50:23). Where the Lord is, we always find rest and peace.

The Psalmist reminds himself that even though he is overwhelmed, his boundary lines have fallen in pleasant places, his heritage is beautiful, and his flesh will dwell securely. These are declarations of hope. In his mind's eye, he sees the Lord continually before Him and declares the promise. Though the circumstances may not change, our destiny in God will never fall by the wayside. In this promise, we can be glad.

When was the last time you looked around and experienced gladness swell in your heart? When was the last time your soul burst with singing solely because the Lord is good? Do we experience these moments only in the enjoyable seasons, or can we begin to enter into these moments in the desperate and turbulent times? When we can come into His courts with praise and thanksgiving in the weakest and lowly times, our love matures.

It is, in fact, a mature love that Jesus longs for. Rejoice in who He is today. Let gladness swell in your heart. Let your flesh rest in the hope that He never fails and is always the same yesterday and today. Just as the Psalmist, turn the worship music on, rejoice in Him anyway, and see the Lord before you. Because He is there and still seated on the throne, life does not have to rattle your joy. Your flesh can rest in hope.

Reflection:

1. What are you thankful for today?

2. Spend some time praising God for He is. Write down the thoughts that come to your mind.

3. What areas of your life need hope restored?

4. Are you confident that your boundary lines have fallen in pleasant places? How can you rejoice over the boundary lines and the inheritance God has given you?

Activation Prayer:

I praise you today, Jesus, for who you are and how you love me. You see me when I rise and when I fall. You see every fear, worry, and anxious thought. I invite your peace into my heart and mind. Lead me into your courts with praise and thanksgiving. I find my hope and rest in you, Jesus.

Journal:

Day 15

The Helper

"I will ask the Father, and He will give you another Helper, that He may be with you forever."

John 14:16 (NAS)

Read John 14:16-31

The Holy Spirit walks with us, talks with us, and abides in us. He prays when we do not know what to pray. He comforts when there are no words another person can give. He never leaves, always understands, and faithfully points us back to the Father. Today, I encourage you to get to know the Holy Spirit more. Ask Him to refill you, refresh you, and overflow from you.

When we are weary, burdened, and tired, the Holy Spirit is faithful to come. Jesus said it was better for Him to leave us and go to the Father, SO THAT the Holy Spirit could come and be with us. Although Jesus was and is God, He took on flesh as a man on the earth. His presence could not be with us always. He could not abide in us the way the Holy Spirit can.

We so often underestimate the role of the Holy Spirit in our lives. We may be scared or unaware of the power He brings to our lives. When you gave your life to Jesus, the Spirit was offered to you as a free gift. His presence is with you. But, there is more.

The scriptures say that we can also be baptized in the Holy Spirit, meaning He has free reign to move within us and exude power from us. When we are baptized and filled with the Spirit, the presence of God finds its home in us. Where God is, there is rest, peace, stillness, and power.

The Holy Spirit living in us teaches us all things and brings to remembrance Jesus' words (John 14:26). In every circumstance, we have the choice to yield to the Holy Spirit. We get a direct line to Heaven when we are in need of wisdom. When we do not know whether to turn to the right or to the left, we will hear a voice saying this is the way walk in it (Is. 30:21).

A life walking hand in hand with the Holy Spirit is available to us. He is intensely intimate. He knows both everything about you and everything about Jesus. He knows what our heart longs for and the way to the Lord to find it. Therefore, He leads very well and is a friend we can trust.

Reflection:

1. Do you have a moment in your life, when you know you were filled and baptized in the Holy Spirit? If so, write it down as a thankful declaration. If not, I encourage you to pray for it now.

2. What are tangible ways you can sense the help of the Holy Spirit in your life?

3. What is one way you can lean on the Holy Spirit today and trust His wisdom?

4. How can you increase your ability to recognize and hear the voice of the Holy Spirit in your life?

Activation Prayer:

God, I ask you to fill me with your Spirit today. I long for you to find a home in me. Fill me with your presence and power. Help me to walk, talk, and breathe by the Spirit. Thank you for the free gift of your presence.

Journal:

Day 16
Abide in the Light

"I have come as Light into the world, so that everyone who believes in Me will not remain in darkness."

John 12:46 (NAS)

Read John 12:27-50

God the Father dwells in unapproachable light, yet Jesus made a way to the Father (1 Tim. 6:16). He is the ultimate atonement for our sins. It is important to remember that sin separates us from God's presence (Is. 59:2). Sin hinders our approach. Even though His mercy and grace cover us, if we live in habitual sin, we welcome darkness into our lives. God can not be one with darkness. Daily we should actively apply the blood of Jesus, ask for His forgiveness, and welcome the kind conviction of the Spirit.

We will all fall short of the glory of God, so we do not have to wait until we are perfect to approach God (Rom. 3:23). We approach Him under the blood and receive His forgiveness so that our sin does not remain. In John chapter 8, Jesus did not condemn the adulteress woman. He brought her near. He also then instructed her to "go, and sin no more" (John 8:11). Jesus is the light that drives out the darkness so that we can draw near to God (John 8:12).

The kingdom of God is advancing, and the violent take it by force (Matt. 11:12). We live in grace and rest in God, yet we violently address sin and confidently speak the gospel. It is good practice to regularly stop and ask Jesus, the light, to shine in our hearts and reveal any wicked way in us (Ps. 139:24). Often when we are living in unrest, there is sin hiding in the shadows. Sin distances us from God. Distance from God brings unrest.

There could be a habitual sin that we are already aware of that needs to be dealt with that is disturbing the peace within us. Sometimes, our sin is as rudimentary as forsaking our first love, Jesus. We become busy and restless when we try to do things in our strength while not addressing sinful habits. Let's take a moment to lay our lives down again before Him, allow Him to search our hearts, and reveal any place in our lives where He does not have full reign. Jesus is light. Let Him shine. He has a home of rest for you called His mercy and forgiveness.

Reflection:

1. Ask the Lord to search your heart. Write down any area(s) of your life that need to receive His forgiveness and light.

2. If you are forgiven of your sins, how then does this impact your daily walk?

3. Do you violently and intentionally reject sin in your life, or is sin dealt with lightly?

4. Frequently, God asks us to confess our sins to one another to be healed (James 5:16). Is there a safe person in your life to confess your sin?

Activation Prayer:

Jesus, come and shine your light in me. I humble myself before you and repent of any wicked way in me. I desire for you to live in and through me. Thank you for your blood spilled out for the atonement of my sins. I receive your grace and mercy.

Journal:

Day 17

Abide in the Shadow

"He who dwells in the shelter of the Most High will abide in the shadow of the Almighty."

Psalm 91:1 (NAS)

Read Psalm 91

Yesterday, we focused on abiding in Jesus, the light. His light shines in the darkness and uncovers everything that keeps us separated from Him. Today, we are focusing on abiding in the shadow. I am not referring to a shadow of darkness, rather the shadow of the Almighty. When someone is standing near or over you, they block the heat from the sun's rays or the darts from the enemy line. He stands as our protector from the enemy's fiery darts. He is a shield before and behind us.

He is powerful to withstand the enemy and all-knowing. It is His job to know when and how the enemy might try to come against us. It is our job to dwell in the secret place. We remain still and hide in His shadow. It is wise to stay close. We do not go our way or at our choice speed. Following Jesus is an intimate journey. We take one step at a time while intentionally remaining in our place of refuge.

It makes me think of a young daughter standing on her Father's shoes as they waltz around a dance floor. His face is beaming with joy. Her smile stretches from one ear to the other. She trusts him, she follows him, and she would never imagine jumping off. Her joy springs forth in the dance. She remains in his shadow.

The secret place with God is a quiet place where confidential conversations unfold. It is a safe place where we can make our home. Deciding to stay near to the Lord and abide in His shadow is the wisest decision we can ever make. No matter where life takes us, His shadow is our safe place. He always has your back. Where fear, anxiety, distrust, or discontentment has set in, allow God to display His faithfulness to you. He never leaves us or forsakes us (Deut. 31:6). Even in the waiting, He is always there. He is always the same.

Imagine yourself jumping on your Heavenly Father's shoes. Trust Him in the dance, remain in His shadow, lean on His strength, and delight in who you are to Him.

Reflection:

1. Write down the verse that speaks to you the most in Psalm 91. Claim it as a promise from God.

2. What are two ways God has displayed His faithfulness to you?

3. How is the encouragement to abide in the shadow of the Almighty comforting to you?

4. How can you jump on your daddy's shoes today and enjoy the waltz?

Activation Prayer:

Lord, I thank you for the peace, stillness, and protection that remains in your shadow. Help me stay near to you and in step with your Spirit. Thank you that I find my home in you. I praise you for your faithfulness to meet me.

Journal:

Day 18

Abide in the Vine

"Abide in me, and I in you. As the branch cannot bear fruit of itself unless it abides in the vine, so neither can you unless you abide in me."

John 15:4 (NAS)

Read John 15:1-11

The word *abide* beckons us to remember its incredible importance. We abide in the light, we abide in His shadow, and we abide in the vine. In John 15, Jesus compares Himself to a vine and us to branches. Everything we do and everything we are stems from Him. We are lost and empty without Him. All efforts and successes are worthless if they are apart from Him. We live in an age where many of us can partner with wise men or technology to get a job done well.

Many people in our society have convinced themselves that they do not need God. This belief aligns with a humanistic mindset and will always fail us. Any lasting fruit worth bearing can only come from Jesus. We may gain success in this world, yet are we bearing good fruit? The fruit that comes from the Heavenly vine is always full of righteousness, peace, joy, faithfulness, and love (Gal. 5:22).

Abiding in the vine for you and I could mean realistically prioritizing time for reading the Bible and in prayer. God has divine wisdom, heavenly blueprints, and kingdom creativity waiting for you to lay hold off. There are practical ways to help you abide even if you don't have hours to give every day. Perhaps playing worship music while you wash dishes or listening to a sermon while you answer emails will help you keep your eyes on the Lord.

Fruit that comes from Jesus is fruit that does not grow bitter, is more generous than we could have imagined, and sweeter than our hands could ever make. Abiding in the vine means yielding to His lead and allowing Him to do the heavy lifting.

Abiding in the vine means that no matter where we are called to go or what we are called to do, we remain in Him. There is no success worth achieving if it requires us to detach ourselves from the vine. We might have to walk away from opportunities the world offers that do not bear godly fruit or align with the world's system. Choosing holiness is part of the Christian walk. We learn to live in the world but not be of the world. We find rest in abiding.

Although the world's pleasures might be tempting and even pleasurable for a moment, they will never last. The wages of sin are always death (Rom. 6:23). Abide in the vine, and you will always receive life. If your efforts and daily responsibilities are not life-giving, perhaps stepping back and asking for God's perspective might help. He may even instruct you to lay something down to rest.

Reflection:

1. What is a practical way you can "abide in the vine" today?

2. Are your times with the Lord what you wish they could be? If not, how can you prioritize them more or be creative to find time?

3. Is there an area in your life that you have been trying to live on your own? Will you take some time to give it back to God?

4. Is there anything you are giving your time and efforts to today that perhaps Jesus might be asking you to lay down to breathe life back into you?

Activation Prayer:

Jesus, I praise you for being my vine. Thank you for the fruit you have produced in me. I pray that you will continue to create fruit in my life that will last and bear your name. I lay down all my striving, strengths, and talents before you.

Journal:

Day 19

Abide in His Word

"If you abide in me, and my words abide in you, ask whatever you
wish, and it will be done for you."

John 15:7 (NAS)

Read John 15:1-11

The Word of God became flesh, and He lived and dwelt among us. I
can only imagine what it would have been like to sit under Jesus'
teaching face to face or in the grass as He preached in the open air.
The gift it was to hang on every word that proceeded from His
mouth. Although He is not sitting among us in the flesh, His Word is
still living and active (Heb. 4:12). A life abiding in His Word is a
life consumed with promise, trust, and destiny. His words are life-
giving. His words speak truth to our hearts and souls. His promises
are always "yes and amen" (2 Cor. 1:20).

The words that come from His mouth demand life, honor, and favor.
By one word, He spoke light into existence. This powerful voice is
the same voice that speaks life into our personal lives. With one

word from His mouth, He can call things that are not present to existence.

Jesus says if we abide in Him and His words abide in us, the godly desires of our hearts will be done. No dream is too big for God or no task too hard that cannot receive supernatural assistance from Heaven. When we abide in Him, answered prayers are a regular occurrence and angels are sent to propel us into our destiny. Can you imagine? Do you live this way? Our present circumstances do not determine our future, God's dreams for us determine our future. A wise mentor of mine often says, "You are God's dream wrapped in flesh." It is our joy to walk out His dreams.

He hears the prayers of His righteous ones, those who live according to the Word of God (Prov. 15:29). Our righteousness is found in Him, not in our good works (1 Cor. 1:30). Abide in Him, let His truth abide in you, and you will fulfill your God-ordained destiny. You will find rest for your souls absent from striving. He will be the lamp unto your feet and the light unto your path (Ps. 119:105).

Reflection:

1. I encourage you to meditate on John 15:7 and write down anything the Lord speaks to you.

2. What is one consistent prayer of yours that is still unanswered? Pray for it again now full of faith.

3. Are you content with where you are in God? Ask Him for more today.

4. Where you feel weak and underqualified, ask God to come and bestow His favor, strength, and instruction. Write down your prayer.

Activation Prayer:

Jesus, I want to hang on every word that comes from your mouth. Revive me today. Help me seek you with all my heart. Breathe on my desire to read your Word. Thank you that you hear my prayers and want to give me the desires of my heart. Help me to trust you, cease from striving, and rest in your wisdom.

Journal:

Day 20

In His House

"Surely goodness and lovingkindness will follow me all the days of
my life, and I will dwell in the house of the Lord forever."

Psalm 23:6 (NAS)

Read Psalm 23

In God's house, everything is available to His children. When we
are weak, strength is found in His presence. When we are tired and
weary, rest is always accessible. Surely, His goodness follows us all
the days of our lives. As the psalmist says, "One day in His house is
better than a thousand elsewhere" (Ps.84:10). Can you imagine what
life would be like if we were aware of His goodness on our trail
every moment? He is looking for an opportunity to display it. I can
just imagine the Father rejoicing saying, "Yes, I get to show my
goodness to her again." It is as if He is waiting around every corner
with a blessing.

So often we think we have failed God or have not measured up. Perhaps we have sinned again, yelled at our kids, or ate that extra donut we said we wouldn't. (Not that there is anything wrong with donuts). Even if we know the lies are false, we somehow live as if we are performing for God. God does not give us a thumbs up or down based on performance. His mercy follows us. When we fall, He is already there to help us back up or catch us. When we mess it all up, He bends down and helps us pick up the pieces.

There is nothing we can do to make Him love us any more than He already does. To think His kingdom works any different would diminish the work on the cross. His house is our house. Everything in His home has been made available to us. We are His children. Can you imagine owning a beautiful mansion full of toys and telling your (or someone else's) children they are not allowed to explore or play? God does not do this to us. He welcomes us in. He gives us all He has available and blesses us beyond imagination.

We all have days when it is hard to believe that everything is available to us. Prayers are still unanswered, confusion has set in, or even disappointment has made us heartsick. If this is you, meditate on this Psalm. The Psalmist, in fact, was declaring a truth that perhaps he was not experiencing in the moment. We declare truth regardless of what our feelings tell us. Feelings lie. God never lies. Surely, there is goodness to experience today.

Reflection:

1. How has God displayed His goodness to you?

2. In what ways can you actively look for His goodness?

3. In what ways can you live your life displaying His goodness to others?

4. Is there a resource in God's house available to you that you have yet to pick up and claim as your own? Pick it up and claim it.

Activation Prayer:

Thank you, Jesus, for your sacrifice on the cross. Because of your mercy, I can live freely in your house. Help me to see your goodness displayed in my life every day. Open my eyes to see you moving on my behalf. I want to live a life of thankfulness and gratitude as your daughter.

Journal:

Day 21

In His Presence

"One thing I have asked from the Lord, that I shall seek: that I may dwell in the house of the Lord all the days of my life, to behold the beauty of the Lord and to meditate in his temple."

Psalm 27:4 (NAS)

Read Psalm 27

David sings this audacious song. One thing He desires from the Lord. If you were to boil down all the prayers you have prayed throughout your walk with God to one thing, would this be it? Although David's life was in danger, all of His prayers came down to one: to behold the beauty of the Lord and live in His presence. David understood something paramount. He knew that if He remained near to God, God would take care of everything else. Yes, he still prayed other prayers, but they all rested on this foundation.

He was a man after God's heart. He longed to know intimately the God He served and the God that saw His faithfulness in the pastures. I am sure He was exhausted. He was running from Saul who wanted to kill Him. He also carried kingship as a prophetic promise in his heart. I am sure there were times that he recognized that the prophetic word for his life and his daily circumstances did not quite measure up. His prayers could have easily all rested upon His desire to stay alive or on His desire for God to hurry up and make him king. We might have even understood if these were his primary desires. Nevertheless, His prayer was not to live in the King's house but to live in the King of King's house. He had a higher vision.

It is difficult to fathom the beauty of the Lord and what it would be like to behold it. David's prayer reminds me of Moses' prayer for just a glimpse of His glory (Ex. 33:18). The Lord's beauty is overwhelming, so He gives us glimpses. For example, we see His beauty in each other. Every person is His creation exudes a facet of God. We see it if we take the time to behold it.

We see His beauty in all His creation. The trees, the stars, the mountains, and the oceans all display a part of who He is. I often wonder if David sang this song as a response to His heart's desire for godly perspective. When darkness and exhaustion are closing in, just a glimpse of the beauty of the Lord changes everything.

Practically, beauty and rest can be found in a quick trip to the beach, a date night, or one night alone in a hotel room. There is just something about taking a step back in a busy season to breathe and soak up beauty around you: it shifts everything.

Reflection:

1. Where do you see God's beauty in your life?

2. List 2-3 people that display a facet of God's character to you?

3. Do you need God to give you a fresh perspective?

4. If all your prayers boiled down to one central prayer, what would that prayer be?

Activation Prayer:

Jesus, I want to behold your beauty. I ask for eyes to see it all around me. Give me a fresh godly perspective on my circumstances and help me to rest in your goodness.

Journal:

Day 22

Cultivate Faithfulness

"Trust in the Lord, and do good; dwell in the land and cultivate faithfulness. Delight yourself in the Lord, and He will give you the desires of your heart."

Psalm 37:3-4 (NAS)

Read Psalm 37

We do not perform for God, yet our faithfulness counts. God saw David tending His sheep in the field. He took note of his faithfulness and exalted him. David was a man who truly loved God and was found trustworthy with more. His mundane tasks mattered to God. Your daily mundane tasks matter to God. Your heart matters. Your integrity matters. You matter. When you feel unnoticed, passed by, or underappreciated, God sees it all. His opinion is the only important one at the end of the day. Delight yourself in the Lord and cultivate faithfulness where you are today. That is the best you can do. He will take care of tomorrow.

His Word promises that if you delight yourself in Him, He will not ignore the desires of your heart. In fact, He is the one who gives us the desires. They are not to fool or tempt us. Your longings are there so you can entrust them to Him. It is often difficult to resist the urge to strive, show ourselves approved before men, or even step on someone else to get where we want to go. Nevertheless, God exalts the humble (Luke 14:11).

God is looking for the one mopping the kitchen floor faithfully. He sees the one handling her business or home finances with integrity. He takes note of the mom waking up with little ones faithfully in the night. These are His children in whom are all His delight. He cultivates faithfulness, trust, and discipline in us in the mundane tasks. He uses our daily responsibilities to instruct us and prepare us for the next step.

The mundane is extremely important and purposeful. Don't despise it. He gets you ready and positioned so that when an opportunity comes along, He can look at you as one who has studied and shown yourself approved. He looks at the moment and says, "Yes. I know just the daughter to entrust this to." Let your roots go deep today and be faithful. Even if no one else notices or appreciates you, your faithfulness matters to God.

Reflection

1. Where has God called you to be faithful?

2. What are the desires of your heart? Pray them back to God.

3. Think of ways you can dwell in your land today rather than worrying about the future.

4. What circumstances in your life test your faithfulness, integrity, or consistency? Can you see God using these circumstances to prepare you for more responsibility?

Activation Prayer:

Jesus, I praise you for the ways you care for me. Thank you that I am not unnoticed. You have never forgotten me and will never forsake me. Help me to serve you with my whole heart. I want to cultivate faithfulness in my life. I trust you with my desires, my hopes, and my dreams. Thank you that you hold my heart in your hand and care for it well.

Journal:

Day 23

Eternal Perspective

"And I heard a great voice out of heaven saying, 'Behold, the tabernacle of God is with men, and He will dwell with them, and they shall be His people. God Himself will be with them and be their God."

Revelation 21:3 (NKJV)

Read Revelation 21

One day we will see Him face to face, and He will wipe away every tear, remove every burden, and fully restore us to Him. We will be the Bride we long to be. Our eyes can focus on eternity with expectation and desire. Living with an eternal perspective reminds us that this world is not our home. We make the best of it and serve with excellence, yet this is just the beginning of our walk with the Lord.

If you know and love Jesus as your Lord and Savior, you have much to look forward to. A mentor of mine always reminds me that this life is simply our internship. Eternity is when it gets exceptional. Of course, our wait creates a tension in our hearts. We long for the day we will be with Jesus, yet we can also live in joy and peace in the present. We learn to cultivate faithfulness in the mundane and long for the supernatural of Heaven.

One day soon, God will dwell with us in His fullness, and all of Heaven and earth will rejoice. Our present circumstances are temporary. Although our world feels like it is spinning at times, we can rest in the knowledge that Jesus will return. It is imminent. He will establish His kingdom on the earth, and we will be His forever (Luke 1:33). We can rest in this. Nothing can alter His plans, no matter how many times we feel we have failed Him.

Our job is to yield to Him and fulfill the assignments He gives us today. Remember, He is good, and He is coming back to make everything right. Living with an eternal perspective changes the way that we live. When we are tempted to build our kingdom on the earth, eternity reminds us that we do not get to take it with us. Let's put our energy, our strength, our time, and our passions into a life that has eternal significance.

You do not have to be famous or have a platform to make an eternal impact. Raising your children in the admonition of the Lord, serving with excellence, and investing in your relationships all demonstrate the heart of Jesus. He is not coming back for a bride that performed well. He is coming for a bride that looks like Him.

Reflection:

1. Do you think about eternity? When you think about it, what questions do you have?

2. What do you think it will feel like to look at Jesus face to face as His bride?

3. How might your life be different if lived in excitement for eternity?

4. What can you give yourself to today that will bear eternal fruit?

Activation Prayer:

Thank you for my assignment on the earth today. Thank you for those you have called me to serve, lead, and lay my life down for. I long to serve with excellence. Unite my perspective with yours. Give me a heart that waits in expectation for you. I want to live with an eternal perspective.

Journal:

Day 24

Jehovah Jireh

"Even the sparrow has found a home, and the swallow a nest for herself, where she may have her young— a place near your altar, Lord Almighty, my King and my God."

Psalm 84:3 (NIV)

Read Psalm 84

My God will supply all your needs (Phil. 4:19). He loves to give gifts to His children (Matt. 7:11), and He owns the all cattle on the hill (Ps. 50:10). These are truths and declarations for you today. Many of us already know these verses, yet live as if they are not true. He is our Jehovah-Jireh, our provider. Even the sparrow finds a home in Him. Even the birds of the air and the grass in the ground trust in Him to provide. He is the one who created them all, and He is the one who sustains them. He loves all of His creation, yet we are the ones made to be in relationship with Him. Therefore, how much more can we trust in Him to provide for us (Matt. 7:11)?

I love this picture of the sparrow making her nest for her young. She diligently collects all she needs and carefully constructs her nest.

She is excellent in what she does, yet she rests and enjoys what is provided for her. She works hard, but she rests in the secure place near the Lord. She knows He has a good plan for her and her family. She is confident in His plan and experiences no lack. She reminds me of the Proverbs 31 woman.

Just as a sparrow's nest, everything has been provided for us to curl up, get close, and rest secure. We may go through seasons when the wind blows, the rains fall, and we even have to regather our supplies for our nest, but God never leaves or changes. He is like the tree for the sparrow that remains. The roots grow deep and consistently provide a place for her to make a home. Although He is mighty and the Creator of it all, He cares. On this foundation is where we want to build our nest. A home constructed on sand will blow over when the winds come. But, a house built on the rock will stand in any storm (Matt. 7:24).

He is our provider. We work hard and with excellence, but He is the one that ultimately provides for us. We do not put our trust in man, a job, a career, our intelligence, or even our expertise. Although these are all good things, we trust in the living God who cares for us deeply. Jobs change. Circumstances change. God never changes.

Reflection:

1. On what foundation are you building your house?

2. Are there times in your life when it is difficult to trust in God's provision?

3. What kind of season are you in now? How can you begin or continue to make your nest near the Lord's altar?

4. How do you relate to the mother sparrow?

Activation Prayer:

Jesus, I praise you that I have been fearfully and wonderfully created. You created me to be near to you, and it is your delight to provide for all of my needs. You can provide beyond my expectations. You care about the details of my life and the worries of my heart. Help me to rest in you and find my home in you. I want to build my house on a godly foundation.

Journal:

Day 25

Stillness

"Be still, and know that I am God; I will be exalted among the
nations, I will be exalted in the earth."

Psalm 46:10 (NIV)

Read Psalm 46

Stillness takes practice. Our world bombards us with worries,
unrealistic expectations, and comparisons. It takes time and
diligence to quiet our mind and still our physical body. But, God
encourages us and even commands us to remain still before Him.
How can we stay seated in the middle of the hustle and bustle
around us? How can we be still with little ones begging at our toes?
How can we be still when our boss has expectations beyond our
time and resources? These are the daily demands we all face. God's
exhortation remains.

Stillness is a posture of our heart. It can also be a concerted effort to
rest from busyness. Stillness may look different for you than it does
for me. But, I love that God follows His exhortation with a
reminder, "I WILL be exalted in the earth." We need to be reminded

of this promise when our world seems to be in trouble. We trust in His sovereignty. The world's circumstances or our daily circumstances do not move Him. Nothing creates worry in the heart of God. He is in control and wants to deliver us from fear.

We can get caught up in all that is going wrong with our world and not remember who God is. He is the King of Kings and the Lord of Lords. Even scoffers do not faze Him. His heart breaks for those that are turning away from Him and mistreating His Bride, but He knows that He will still win the war. He will be exalted in the earth, and He wants to be lifted up in our life. It is a compelling testimony to the world to see believers at rest when the storm is raging. We can be still and live with joy in our hearts even in the most burdensome situations. It is a powerful way to live.

Reflection:

1. How can you be still before the Lord today?

2. Is there someone in your life that needs to see your rest and joy in the midst of trials?

3. What is your testimony? I encourage you to write it down and reflect on what God has done and what He plans to do in your life.

4. How do you find rest? What helps you to relax? Do that today as you meditate on the heart of God for you.

Activation Prayer:

Jesus, I exalt you as King in my life. Thank you that I can have peace and stillness even when the world around me is spinning. Help me to keep my eyes on you and not my present circumstances. I desire my life to be a living testimony to your power, peace, and joy.

Journal:

Day 26

His Nearness

"Seek the Lord while He may be found; call upon Him while He is near."

Isaiah 55:6 (NAS)

Read Isaiah 55

Life is not about what we can do for God; it is all about what we get to do it with God. The prophet Isaiah understood this, David understood this as He sought the Lord's beauty, and even Peter understood this as He preached His first sermon following the outpouring of the Holy Spirit on the early church. The Lord draws near to those who draw near to Him (Ps. 145:18). He is a kind gentleman who will not suddenly approach us and overwhelm us. He waits for even the smallest glimpse to come His way. When our eyes turn toward Him, His heart leaps and His pursuit increases. Often, when we become restless, lonely, overwhelmed, or even depressed, we have transferred our gaze from God to ourselves.

Seeking the Lord is an intentional pursuit. We find Him when our hands remain on the pages of our Bible, our eyes gaze at Jesus' red letters, and our spirit is engaged in constant prayer. The pursuit of God is an intentional life-long discipline. In reality, there may be seasons when He is harder to find, yet it does not mean He is absent (Jer. 29:13). The worries of this life cloud our perception of Him. The haze and fog increase even though He is still nearby.

There are days when all my kids want to play hide and seek over and over again. We laugh because although my 3-year old loves the game, she is not very good at staying hidden. She is tiny, so she is hard to find. But, she is so full of excitement that she gives my older kids hints while they search so they will discover her faster. They know that if they call her name enough times, she will jump out and say, "Here I am." They get her every time, and every time she jumps out with a contagious smile never knowing she lost the game.

The other day as we played hide and seek, I watched my daughter as her little body squirmed in her hiding place. I watched her face light up as her siblings found her. It made me think of the kindness of the Lord. Although He doesn't play hide and seek with us, I imagine Him on the edge of His seat waiting for us to open our eyes to see Him right in front of us. Just like my daughter, He wants to be found. The nearness of God is our good (Ps. 73:28). Stay near to God and the fog will decrease.

Reflection:

1. What does an intentional pursuit of God look like in your life today?

2. How can you search for God in the midst of your daily responsibilities and demands?

3. What reasons might tempt you to try to "do life" without God's help?

4. Are there situations in your life that seem to cloud God's nearness? What are they? Pray for clarity.

Activation Prayer:

Thank you, God, for always staying close. Even when I can't feel you or see you, I trust that you are holding my hand. But, I ask you to make me more aware of you today. I want to see you working in my life today. Help me be aware and expect your interventions and surprises.

Journal:

Day 27

Fruitfulness

"Where can I go from Your Spirit? Or where can I flee from Your presence? If I ascend to heaven, you are there; if I make my bed in Sheol, behold, you are there. If I take the wings of the dawn, if I dwell in the remotest part of the sea, even there your hand will lead me, and your right hand will lay hold of me."

Psalm 139:7-10 (NAS)

Read Psalm 139

The Psalmist understood the Lord's omnipresence. He understood there was nowhere He could go, even to death itself, that God would not still have His eye on Him. Many of us have experienced trauma, disappointment, and failures. In fact, these are all a part of life. During these times, it is easy to forget about God's presence. Our confusion brings questions, and our heart-break develops doubt. Our flesh and emotions so easily sway in the waves of our current circumstances. These moments are real, and they are often extremely painful.

I am reminded of this Psalmist's revelation often in times of uncertainty. There is nowhere we can go that would cloud God's vision or His ability to comfort us. Also, we now live according to a new covenant. We can not only dwell in the presence of God, but His presence also dwells within us. The Holy Spirit has set up shop in our human frames, and the doubt, fear, or uncertainty that creeps into our mind do not intimidate Him. As real as the situation is, the Lord desires our conversation with Him in the midst of it to be just as real. Even when He is the One with whom we are offended, we can still come.

I have had moments when I could relate to Peter in John 6:67-68. At this time in the scriptures, we learn that many of Jesus' followers were falling away. Many of them were counting the cost of following Him and deciding the price tag was too high. Perhaps there were some that were offended, exhausted, confused, or even just ready for life to be "normal" again.

Jesus turns to His twelve disciples and asks, "You do not want to go away also, do you?" Immediately, Peter's response jumps right to the truth they all need to hear. Peter responds, "Lord, to whom shall we go? You have words of eternal life." Peter was human and imperfect just like you and me. He often doubted, feared, and even rejected Jesus. But, when the rubber met the road, He understood there was nowhere else to go that would satisfy as Jesus satisfies. When we are tired, worn out, and want to quit, He remains.

Reflection:

1. Are there circumstances in your life that have clouded your sight of Jesus?

2. Ask God to give you the ability to see Him today, and record where you saw glimpses of Him.

3. Jesus said He is the bread of life. Are there other things, places, or people you turn to satisfy your hungry soul? How can you turn back to Jesus for true satisfaction?

4. How can you relate to Peter's declaration today?

Activation Prayer:

God, I praise you today for your never-ending pursuit. Thank you that no matter where I go, or what I do, you see me and are intimately acquainted with all of my ways. You are the bread of life. No one else satisfies as you satisfy. Help me to turn to you for my comfort, satisfaction, and reassurance. Fill me up today and equip me to serve you with joy.

Journal:

Day 28

Planted

"Blessed is the man who trusts in the Lord and whose trust is in the Lord. For he will be like a tree planted by the water, that extends its roots by a stream and will not fear when heat comes; but its leaves will be green, and it will not be anxious in a year of drought nor cease to yield fruit."

Jeremiah 17:7-8 (NAS)

Read Jeremiah 17:1-8

It matters where a tree is planted. A tree planted in a desert struggles for nourishment. It might even wither and die in seasons of drought. This tree is dependent on daily refreshing for its life. Living life in abundance might be a constant struggle. On the other hand, the tree planted by the stream knows its permanent water source. It is just as dependent on the rain, but the refreshing remains. The water source for this tree never runs dry. The tree by the water is not barely getting by in life; it is satisfied.

This comparison demonstrates the difference between running to the world for satisfaction and depending on God. The world might provide a temporary fix, but it will always come up short. A life planted in Jesus will never fall short. Even in a season of drought, the life abiding in Jesus bears lasting fruit. It does not fear the heat, and its leaves remain green as its roots go deeper into the nourished soil.

Paul reminds us in Philippians 4:6 to relinquish all anxiety and present our requests to the Lord. Daily trusting God is a life of faith. Our faith reminds us that we are planted by a stream that never runs dry. Even when the heat comes, our leaves stay green. When we take our eyes off the Lord and become dependent on ourselves, we dry up quickly. When we remain rooted in the soil next to the stream, the peace of God surpasses our understanding and guards our hearts and minds (Phil. 4:7).

Jesus reminds us, just as He did the woman at the well, "Everyone who drinks this water will be thirsty again, but whoever drinks the water I give them will never thirst. Indeed, the water I give them will become in them a spring of water welling up to eternal life" (John 4:13-14). Jesus' water never runs dry. It daily produces life and fruit. Let's be like the Samaritan woman who abandoned her water pot, drank in Jesus, and started revival in our hometown. The same woman who has previously felt defeated experiences a spiritual awakening when she finally understands who her true water source is.

Reflection:

1. How can you plant yourself next to "the stream" today?

2. Can you imagine living without anxiety and always bearing fruit? How can you walk into this reality today?

3. What are your requests to God today?

4. What does it mean for you to leave your water pot at the well and choose Jesus?

Activation Prayer:

God, I praise you for who you are and who you have called me to be. Thank you that you have not overlooked me, but I have everything I need to bear fruit that remains. I want to plant myself in you. Help me be dependent on you today. I give you my worries and anxieties, and I present my requests to you with a thankful heart.

Journal:

Day 29

Soaring

"Even youths grow tired and weary, and young men stumble and fall, but those who hope in the Lord will renew their strength. They will soar on wings like eagles; they will run and not grow weary, they will walk and not faint."

Isaiah 40:30-31 (NIV)

Read Isaiah 40

Even the youngest, the fastest, and the most ambitious among us grow tired and weary. We are all weak and broken people limited by a flesh suit that can only run so fast. We all need rest. But, I love this promise from the Lord in Isaiah. It is possible to run the race and not grow weary. We can walk, even the hardest terrains, and not faint. We can soar. We are feeble, but God is mighty.

When we partner with the Kings of Kings, we become royalty seated in Heavenly places far above the worry, fear, and burdens of this life. We are called a royal priesthood. Peter goes as far to say that we are "God's special possession, that you may declare the praises of Him who called you out of darkness into His wonderful light" (1 Pet. 2:9). A royal priest, a life seated with Christ, lives from a different life source than the world.

We can soar on wings of eagles above the circumstance, gain heavenly perspective, and even declare the Word of the Lord over our uncertain situations. Our refreshing and renewal come from a holy place. Living in this reality is the life God has intended for you. Time does not slow down, yet our perspective and where we draw our strength from can.

Running becomes less about busyness or needing to fill our lives with things that drain us. Running means staying in step with Jesus today, even if it means you need to jump on His back for a ride to rest your legs. (Maybe this is how we run and not grow tired.) Resting in the midst of the piggy-back adventure means we keep our eyes on Jesus not on how fast others are going. Are there ever times when you compare yourself to the fast-paced mom who is running with such grace and ease? Have you ever marveled at a co-worker who always finishes a project with excellence and speed?

These comparisons are draining. Find your speed on the back of Jesus and just enjoy the ride. Don't miss the beauty, thrill, and satisfaction available to you. We miss out on joy when our eyes are looking at someone else's ride. We can soar on the wings of eagles and run without becoming weary when our eyes remain on Jesus. When we take our eyes off of Him and focus them on others, our lack and insecurity fester. Consequently, unrest and exhaustion settle in.

Reflection:

1. What would it be like to actually soar like an eagle? Meditate on this verse and record your thoughts.

2. How might an eagle's perspective of the world from the air be different than ours on the ground? How does this relate to living with a heavenly perspective?

3. I encourage you to move from praying for your needs to declaring God's promises over your life. Write down two declarations for yourself today.

4. What are you running with Jesus to accomplish today?

Activation Prayer:

Jesus, thank you that you have called me a royal priest. You have spoken promises into my life through others and your Word that are mine to claim. Help me to walk in your promises. Jesus, you are my life source. I look to you for strength, rest, and renewal today. I want to run with you and receive all that you have for me.

Journal:

Day 30

Laid Down

"This is how we know what love is: Jesus Christ laid down his life for us. And we ought to lay down our lives for our brothers and sisters."

1 John 3:16 (NIV)

Read 1 John 3

Jesus Christ paid the ultimate sacrifice for us. The message of the cross is the essence of the Christian faith. Without His sacrifice and His resurrection, we would still be distant. It was a part of His plan to bring us closer. He wants us near to Him and in intimate relationship with Him. The Church is the Bride He is coming back for (Rev. 22:17). He is dedicated and will never give up on her. He has already demonstrated love at its highest, and He calls us to activate this same love for others.

I know it may seem strange to end a devotion on rest with a reminder to lay our life down, but I thought it was appropriate given the way Jesus ended His life on the earth. It is easy to go about our day filling it with daily tasks, but it is important to remember why we are here. Even the most mundane assignment done unto the Lord is fulfilling a divine purpose.

If you are a mother, God has gifted you the ability to be Jesus every day to your children. You have sacrificed beyond what many people would believe. If you are a businesswoman, you care about your co-workers and employees. You are sacrificing for them and doing your part to help them succeed. No matter what our daily tasks look like, our calling is all the same. We are destined to know love in its purest form. Love is Jesus. Love is His life laid down.

We rest in the knowledge of who He is. We rest in the desire to become like Him. We lay our heads down in the secret place to find Him, and we lay our lives down for others to live as He lives. This reality describes who you are. You can rest in that. Rest is found not in the absence of living, but it prevails in living for the right reasons.

Reflection:

1. What is your definition of rest?

2. Do you believe that God can continue to give you rest in your daily life?

3. Who are you laying your life down for? Take a moment to thank God for them.

4. Remind yourself of the ways you are committed to seeking rest in your life.

Activation Prayer:

God, thank you for the rest that is available to me in your presence. You are my resting place.

Journal:

Reflection

Thank you for dedicating this short season to the Lord. Diligently seeking rest will be a life-long journey for us all, but I pray you found breakthrough, understanding, and fresh perspective as you gave yourself to find it today.

One last time, I encourage you to pray and dedicate this sweet time to Jesus. Ask Him to seal all He has done and to bring to remembrance in the coming days the truth He has planted in your heart as you walk it out.

Life is hard and often unfair. It exhausts us all at times, but I encourage you to keeping running after Jesus and keep fighting for your resting place in Him. Our life is but a vapor, so live it to the fullest. And on those days you are really tired and worn down, take an extra hour to pull those covers up over your exhausted body, close your eyes, and say, "Thank you, Jesus. I will find rest for my soul today."

About the Author

Cathy Harris lives with her husband and 3 children in Virginia. She homeschools her children, teaches local childbirth classes, and writes books and blog posts in her spare time. She is the author of *Created to Live: Becoming the Answer for an Abortion-Free Community* and writes at cathyharris.org. Juggling all her responsibilities is challenging, but she is determined to find Jesus in it all. Outside of serving her family, Cathy's primary passion is encouraging, teaching, and honoring women along their journey.

For more information about

Cathy Harris

and

Laid Down

please visit:

www.cathyharris.org

www.facebook.com/MaryCatHarris

Instagram: marycatharris

* 9 7 8 0 6 9 2 0 6 7 2 9 1 *